Good Luck!

Inspiring thoughts for new parents

Jenny Clements

Good Luck!

Inspiring thoughts for new parents

Jenny Clements

Andrews McMeel
Publishing

Kansas City

A new baby is like the beginning of all things—wonder, hope, a dream of possibilities.

Eda J. Le Shan

So, you've had

a baby.

It's OK to freak out—millions of parents
have been here before you.

The first step is to

accept

that there are centuries of knowledge
within you, so learn to rely on intuition.

It's OK to sound like an idiot,
so ask lots of

questions.

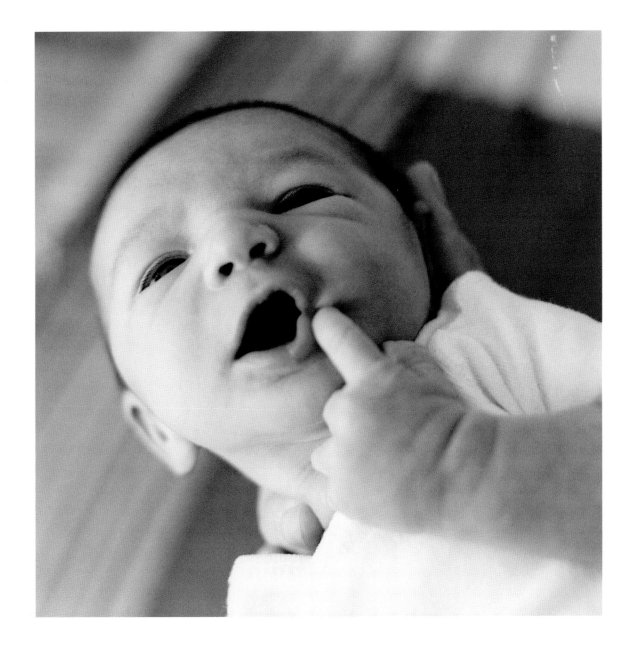

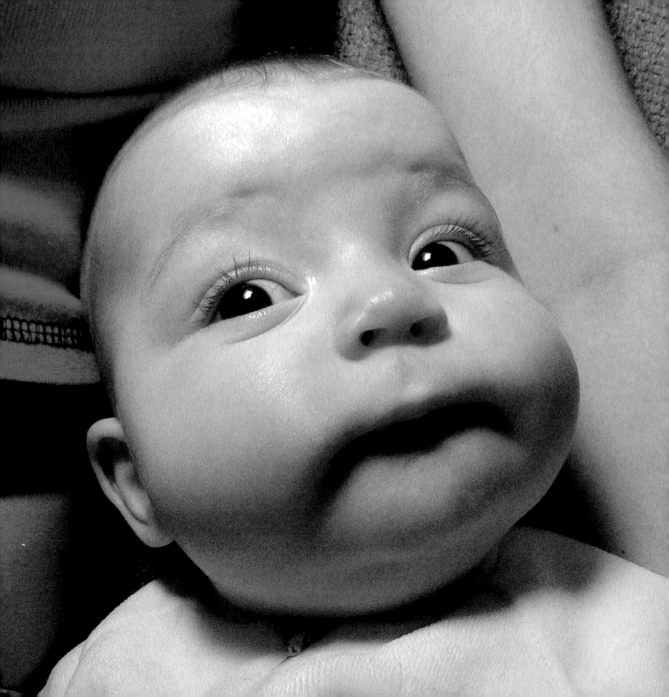

But be

wise

enough to use only the
answers that suit you.

Always

remember

your baby is one of a kind, so every piece
of advice is just a guideline.

Don't worry, in time
your baby will

sleep

through the night, and so will you.

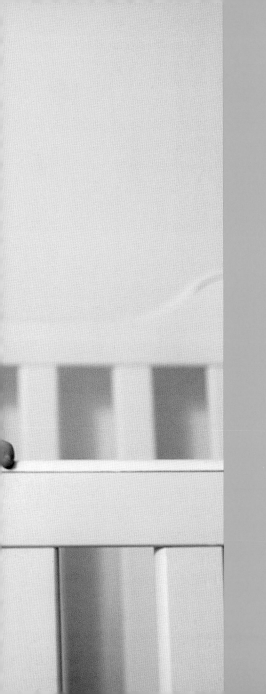

Maybe not all the time . . .

but more often than not.

Experiencing everything for the first time is

wondrous.

Count yourself lucky that you get to relive those
moments through your baby.

It's OK to cry—
most people do.

Keep the love flowing.
What goes around, comes around.

Relish the opportunity to talk

gibberish

and get away with it.

When you need a break,
remember everyone else is
dying for a cuddle.

If in doubt, blame it
on the baby brain.

Always remember that you are dealing with
a little human being, so handle
your baby as you like to be handled:

with care.

Learn from

baby steps.

The more you take, the
more confident you become.

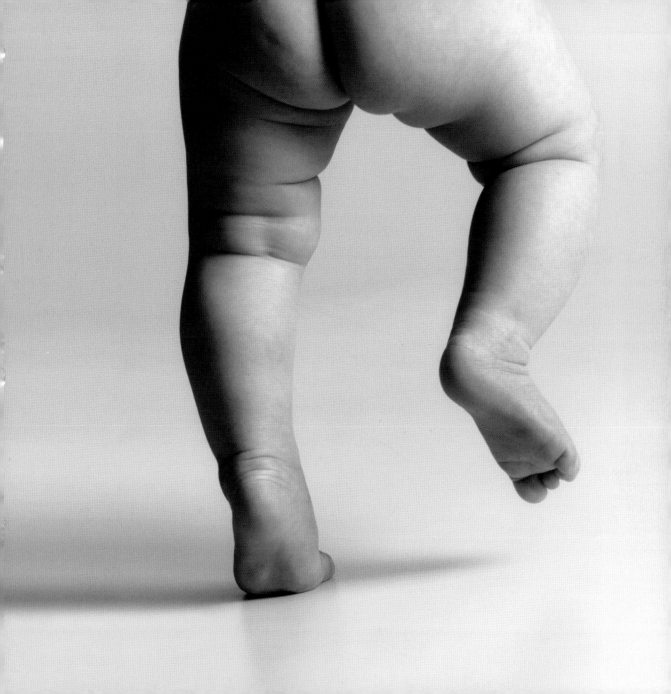

And stay flexible.

Life's one big adventure;

inspire

your baby to reach for the stars.

Be proud.

It's a tough job with
only one reward—your baby.

Most importantly, remember to
keep smiling because everything will be

just fine.

After all, you turned out all right.

This book is dedicated to Jenni Paykel—an inspirational woman, mother, and grandma. Her constant example showed us the importance of being surrounded by laughter, friends, family, and good food, and of embracing everything in life with conviction.

I have the honor of loving her son, Simon, and of bringing Jenni's grandchildren into the world. Her son is a truly amazing and loving dad, living and giving according to his mother's guidance and inspiration.

We miss her every day and hope we make her proud!

Jenni Paykel
September 12, 1944—July 2, 2004

Special thanks to Isla, Julian, Uri, Simon, and the PQ team.
I couldn't have done it without you.

This edition published in 2006 by Andrews McMeel Publishing, an Andrews McMeel Universal company, 4520 Main Street, Kansas City, Missouri, 64111. No part of this publication may be used or reproduced in any manner whatsoever without written permission except in the case of reprints in the context of reviews.

The images in this book are copyright © Getty Images.

The publisher is grateful for literary permissions to reproduce the item below subject to copyright. Every effort has been made to trace the copyright holders and the publisher apologizes for any unintentional omission. We would be pleased to hear from any not acknowledged here and undertake to make all reasonable efforts to include the appropriate acknowledgment in any subsequent editions. *A new baby is like the beginning of all things—wonder, hope, a dream of possibilities.* Extract from *How to Survive Parenthood* by Eda J. Le Shan, Random House, 1965. Reproduced with kind permission from Rosenstone/Wender.

Designed by Cameron Gibb

Printed by Midas Printing International Ltd, China

ISBN-13: 978-0-7407-5770-9
ISBN-10: 0-7407-5770-9

www.andrewsmcmeel.com